Gluten-Free Diet
A Shopping Guide

By James L. Shirley

Printed in the United States of America

First printing: May 2011

ISBN: 978-0615466767

"*Gluten-Free Diet: A Shopping Guide* makes it easy to find gluten-free groceries. The layout of the book helps me quickly find what I need when my celiac granddaughter visits."
-Kathy H. – Colorado Springs, Colorado

"Shopping to prepare a gluten free meal has never been easier. The *Shopping Guide* provides dozens of product options in every section of the local grocery store."
-Dan D'Acquisto – Houston, Texas

"If you find the thought of preparing a gluten-free meal – for yourself or a guest – as terrifying as I did, this book is for you. It's a simple, easy resource for demystifying the entire grocery-to-table process for gluten-free meal making."
-Rebecca M. - Seattle, Washington

For Karen, Grace, and J.P., and our wonderful families

Contents

Aisles: Beverages

Aisles: Baking

Aisles: Canned Foods

Aisles: Dessert-Related

Aisles: Dry Goods

Aisles: Frozen Foods

Aisles: Infant/Toddler Foods

Aisles: Oils, Sauces, and Spreads

Preface

Not all gluten-free products are labeled "gluten-free," partly because no legal standard exists in the United States for what the label "gluten-free" means. Yet more than one in one hundred and thirty three people have celiac disease or avoid eating gluten. This book uncovers nearly two thousand gluten-free products from the most recognized brands in retail grocers.

The gluten-free status of every product listed in this book has been checked with the manufacturer.

Why You Need This Book:

- **It will save you time,** particularly if you are new to the gluten-free diet, but also if you are a seasoned veteran.

- **It will save you money**. Eating gluten-free can be expensive, especially if you are constrained to buying specialty gluten-free products. This book will open up a world of easy-to-find gluten-free products that are easier on your budget.

- **It will give you confidence**. With this book, you can confidently shop in your local grocery store or an unfamiliar store and find products you can trust are gluten-free.

- **My recommendations**. Brands I recommend are noted with three stars (***) after the name. If you are new to the gluten-free diet, cooking for a gluten-intolerant guest, or interested in trying something new, my recommendations will save you time.

The sections in this book are organized to mimic the layout of a grocery store. Also, the index at the back of the book should help you find specific brands quickly. So carry it along on your next grocery trip and see how easy shopping gluten-free can be!

Remember, a product doesn't have to be in this book to be gluten-free. Many items are naturally gluten-free and there are new products being labeled gluten-free every day! Finally, please help me improve this book for future editions by emailing your suggestions to guide@happyglutenfree.com.

WARNING: The information provided in this book was valid at the time of printing. However, ingredients and product offerings change on a regular basis. Take responsibility for your own health and safety. Always check with the manufacturer to ensure any product mentioned in this book is gluten-free.

Tips

- To find out if a product is gluten-free, contact the manufacturer. Thousands of blogs comment on what is or is not gluten-free, but you should always contact the company to confirm for yourself.

- Many manufacturers will list on their websites which products are gluten-free. These lists can commonly be found under Nutritional Information, Allergen Information, or the Frequently Asked Questions (FAQ) page. The FAQ is generally found on the Contact Us page. If you don't find a gluten-free list, email or call the company.

- These common ingredients are generally gluten-free for products *made in the United States*:
    - Whey
    - Monosodium glutamate (MSG)– Note that MSG doesn't settle well for some people with celiac disease.
    - Caramel color
    - Maltodextrin

Tips Cont'd

- Label-reading becomes even more useful if you know the company's stance on labeling gluten ingredients. For example, 'Natural Ingredients' on a Kraft product can be trusted because Kraft labels all gluten-containing ingredients (including barley, rye, and malt).

- Support your local gluten-free bakeries and restaurants!

- Remember, wheat-free does not mean gluten-free!

- Products with statements like, "Manufactured in a facility that also processes wheat" or "Manufactured on equipment that also processes wheat" may be ones you should avoid depending on your sensitivity to gluten.

Perimeter: Produce

Produce

Fresh fruit and vegetables in the produce section of the grocery store are gluten-free. Check the labels on pre-packaged fruit mixes and fruit or vegetable dips since they may have added ingredients. Avoid wheat grass and wheat malt. Also stay away from barley, malt, and oats.

Perimeter: Deli and Meats

(Also see the Aisles: Frozen Meats section)

Deli and Meat Counter

Many meats and cheeses at the deli are gluten-free. However, there is significant threat of cross-contamination with gluten from the slicers, cutting boards, and knives.

Look for pre-sliced, pre-packaged meats and cheeses. Refer to the Lunch Meats and Cheeses sections later in this guide for a variety of gluten-free products.

If you need something from the deli, ask how they can help make sure sliced meats and cheeses can be trusted to be gluten-free. One idea is to be the first person at the deli when it opens since all of the equipment will be freshly cleaned.

Breakfast Meats

Applegate Farms
www.applegatefarms.com; 866-587-5858

Natural Canadian Bacon
Natural Dry Cured Bacon
Natural Peppered Bacon
Natural Chicken and Apple Breakfast Sausage
Natural Chicken and Maple Breakfast Sausage
Natural Chicken and Sage Breakfast Sausage
Natural Sunday Bacon
Natural Turkey Bacon
Organic Sunday Bacon
Organic Turkey Bacon

Boulder Sausage ***
www.bouldersausage.com; 866-529-0595

Breakfast Sausage

Breakfast Meats Cont'd

Farmer John
www.farmerjohn.com; 800-846-7635

Center Cut Bacon
Dry Salt Pork Bacon
Ends & Pieces Bacon
Firehouse Hot Roll Sausage Links
Firehouse Hot Skinless Links
Maple Ends and Pieces Bacon
Old Fashioned Maple Skinless Sausage Links
Old Fashioned Table Brand Bacon
Original Roll Sausage Links
Original Skinless Breakfast Sausage Links
Premium Applewood Bacon
Premium Cracked Peppercorn Bacon
Premium Low Sodium Bacon
Premium Old Fashioned Maple Bacon
Premium Original Chorizo
Premium P C Links Lower Fat
Premium Regular Smoked Bacon
Premium S C Links
Premium Sausage Patties Lower Fat
Premium Spicy Hot Chorizo
Premium Thick Sliced Bacon
Premium Traditional Chorizo
Quick Serve Fully Cooked Bacon
Quick Serve Fully Cooked Sausage Links
Table Brand Bacon
Thick Smoked Bacon

Breakfast Meats Cont'd

Hormel *
www.hormel.com; 800-523-4635

Black Label Bacon
Canadian Style Bacon
Crumbled Sausage
Fully Cooked Bacon
Ham Patties
Little Sizzlers Original Sausage Links and Patties
Microwave Bacon
Range Brand Bacon

Jennie-O Turkey Store
www.jennieo.com; 800-621-3505

Breakfast Bacon
Breakfast Lover's Turkey Sausage
Breakfast Sausage Roll
Extra Lean Turkey Bacon
Fully Cooked Turkey Breakfast Sausage Patties
Fully Cooked Turkey Sausage Breakfast Links
Maple Turkey Breakfast Sausage Links
Turkey Breakfast Sausage Links
Turkey Breakfast Sausage Patties

Breakfast Meats Cont'd

Oscar Mayer
www.oscarmayer.com; 877-535-5666

>   All Bacons
>   All Fully Cooked Bacon

Smithfield
www.smithfield.com

>   Center Cut 40% Lower Fat Bacon
>   Cracked Peppercorn Coated Bacon
>   Paula Deen Hot Pork Sausage
>   Paula Deen Mild Pork Sausage
>   Naturally Hickory Smoked Bacon
>   Paula Deen Sausage Links and Patties
>   Thick Sliced Bacon

Breakfast Meats Cont'd

Wellshire Farms *
www.wellshirefarms.com; 877-467-2331

Chicken Apple Brown & Serve Links
Chicken Apple Sausage Patties
Classic Sliced Dry Rubbed Bacon
Classic Sliced Turkey Bacon
Original Breakfast Patties
Original Skinless Brown & Serve Links
Sliced Black Forest Dry Rubbed Bacon
Sliced Canadian Style Turkey Bacon
Sliced Maple Bacon
Sliced Pancetta Bacon
Sliced Peppered Dry Rub Bacon
Sliced Peppered Dry Rubbed Center Cut Bacon
Applewood Smoked
Sunrise Maple Breakfast Links
Sunrise Maple Breakfast Patties
Thick Sliced Dry Rubbed Pork Bacon
Turkey Maple Sausage Patties
Turkey Maple Skinless Brown & Serve Links
Uncured Beef Bacon

Fish

Bumble Bee
www.bumblebee.com

Chunk White Albacore in Oil or Water
Prime Fillet Solid White Albacore in Water
Prime Fillet Solid White Albacore Low Sodium
in Water
Solid White Albacore in Oil or Water

Chicken of the Sea
www.chickenofthesea.com

All
AVOID Tuna Salad Kits

Starkist
www.starkist.com; 412-323-7400

All Classics in Water or Oil, Gourmet Choice
AVOID Meal Kits and Creations products

General Meats

Always Tender
www.hormel.com; 800-523-4635

Flavored Fresh Beef Peppercorn
Flavored Fresh Pork–Brown Sugar Maple
Flavored Fresh Pork–Citrus
Flavored Fresh Pork–Lemon-Garlic
Flavored Fresh Pork–Mediterranean & Olive Oil
Flavored Fresh Pork–Onion-Garlic
Flavored Fresh Pork–Original
Flavored Fresh Pork–Portabella Mushroom
Flavored Fresh Pork–Roast Flavor
Flavored Fresh Pork–Sun-Dried Tomato
Non Flavored Fresh Beef
Non Flavored Fresh Pork

Applegate Farms ***
www.applegatefarms.com; 866-587-5858

Organic Beef Burgers
Organic Turkey Burgers

General Meats Cont'd

Foster Farms
www.fosterfarms.com; 800-255-7227

    Fresh Natural Chicken
    Fresh Natural Turkey
    Ground Chicken
    Ground Turkey

Hormel
www.hormel.com; 800-523-4635

    All SPAM products

Jennie-O Turkey Store
www.jennieo.com; 800-621-3505

    All Ground Turkey
    All Seasoned Breast Meat
    AVOID Teriyaki Sesame & Ginger
    All Turkey Burgers
    All Unseasoned Breast Meat
    Fully Cooked Italian Style Turkey Meatballs

Sanderson Farms
www.sandersonfarms.com; 800-844-4030

    Fresh Chicken

Holiday Meats

Butterball
www.butterball.com; 800-288-8372

>All turkeys
>**AVOID** Stuffed Turkey

Jennie-O Turkey Store
www.jennieo.com; 800-621-3505

>Fresh Young Turkey
>Premium Basted Young Turkey

Smithfield
www.smithfield.com

>Hickory Smoked Boneless Ham

Hot Dogs/Franks

Applegate Farms
www.applegatefarms.com; 866-587-5858

Natural Beef Hot Dogs
Natural Big Apple Hot Dogs
Natural Chicken Hot Dogs
Natural Turkey Hot Dogs
Organic Beef Hot Dogs
Organic Chicken Hot Dogs
Organic Stadium-Style Hot Dogs
Organic Turkey Dogs
The Great Organic Hot Dog
The Greatest Little Organic Smokey Pork
Cocktail Frank

Ball Park
www.ballparkfranks.com; 800-925-3326

Angus Beef Franks–Original
Ball Park Singles Beef Franks
Beef Franks
Fat Free Beef Franks
Grillmaster Deli Style Beef Franks
Grillmaster Hearty Beef Franks
Lite Beef Franks
Turkey Franks

Hot Dogs/Franks Cont'd

Farmer John
www.farmerjohn.com; 800-846-7635

Dodger Dogs
Premium Beef Franks
Premium Jumbo Beef Franks
Premium Jumbo Meat Wieners
Premium Meat Wieners
Premium Quarter Pounder Beef Franks

Oscar Mayer
www.oscarmayer.com; 877-535-5666

Beef Premium Hot Dogs
Cheese Dogs
Classic and 98% Fat Free Wieners
Classic Cheese Turkey Franks
Classic Light Beef Franks
Classic Turkey Franks
Deli Style Hot Dogs
Jalapeno & Cheddar Franks

Hot Dogs/Franks Cont'd

Wellshire Farms
www.wellshirefarms.com; 877-467-2331

4XL Big Beef Franks
Cheese Franks
Chicken Franks
Cocktail Franks
Old Fashioned Beef Frank
Original Deli Frank
Premium Beef Frank
Turkey Franks

Lunch Meats

Applegate Farms
www.applegatefarms.com; 866-587-5858

Black Forest Ham
Natural Coppa
Natural Genoa Salami
Natural Herb Turkey Breast
Natural Honey & Maple Turkey Breast
Natural Honey Ham
Natural Hot Genoa Salami
Natural Hot Soppressata
Natural Pepperoni
Natural Prosciutto
Natural Roast Beef
Natural Roast Turkey Breast
Natural Slow Cooked Ham
Natural Smoked Turkey Breast
Natural Soppressata
Natural Turkey Bologna
Natural Turkey Salami
Organic Genoa Salami
Organic Herb Turkey Breast
Organic Uncured Ham
Pancetta

Lunch Meats Cont'd

Boar's Head
www.boarshead.com; 888-884-2627

All lunch meats

Buddig
www.buddig.com; 888-633-5684

All lunch meats

Farmer John
www.farmerjohn.com; 800-846-7635

Black Forest Ham
Bologna
Cotto Salami
Ham Roll
Headcheese
Mission Loaf
Original Premium Liverwurst
Premium Braunschweiger
Premium Liverwurst with Bacon
Premium Oven Roasted Turkey Breast
Sliced Cooked Ham

Lunch Meats Cont'd

Hillshire Farms
www.gomeat.com; 800-925-3326

Deli Select Baked Ham
Deli Select Brown Sugar Baked Ham
Deli Select Corned Beef
Deli Select Honey Ham
Deli Select Honey Roasted Turkey Breast
Deli Select Mesquite Smoked Turkey Breast
Deli Select Oven Roasted Chicken Breast
Deli Select Oven Roasted Turkey Breast
Deli Select Pastrami
Deli Select Roast Beef
Deli Select Smoked Chicken Breast
Deli Select Smoked Ham
Deli Select Smoked Turkey Breast

Hormel ***
www.hormel.com; 800-523-4635

All Natural Choice meats

Jennie-O Turkey Store
www.jennieo.com; 800-621-3505

All Pre-Sliced Deli Favorites

Lunch Meats Cont'd

Oscar Mayer
www.oscarmayer.com; 877-535-5666

All lunch meats

Wellshire Farms
www.wellshirefarms.com; 877-467-2331

Sliced Beef Pastrami Round
Sliced Black Forest Ham
Sliced Round Cooked Corned Beef
Sliced Tavern Ham
Sliced Top Round Roast Beef
Sliced Turkey Bologna
Sliced Turkey Ham
Sliced Virginia Brand Deli Ham

Note

Good gluten-free sandwiches are now a reality, thanks to bread from Rudi's Gluten Free Bakery and Udi's Gluten Free Bakery. Check out the Breads section for gluten-free breads.

Sausage

Applegate Farms
www.applegatefarms.com; 866-587-5858

Organic Andouille
Organic Chicken and Apple
Organic Fire Roasted Red Pepper
Organic Pork Andouille
Organic Pork Bratwurst
Organic Pork Kielbasa
Organic Spinach and Feta Sausage
Organic Sweet Italian Sausage

Boulder Sausage ***
www.bouldersausage.com; 866-529-0595

Bratwurst
Chorizo
German Sausage
Hot Italian Sausage
Italian Sausage

Sausage Cont'd

Farmer John
www.farmerjohn.com; 800-846-7635

Hot Louisiana Smoked Sausage
Jalapeno Pepper Premium Rope
Jalapeno Pepper Premium Smoked Sausage
Premium Beef Rope
Premium Polish Sausage
Premium Pork Rope
Red Hots Extra Hot Premium Smoked Sausage

Hillshire Farms
www.gomeat.com; 800-925-3326

Beef Hot Links
Beef Smoked Sausage
CheddarWurst
Hot & Spicy Italian Style Smoked Sausage
Hot Links
Polska Kielbasa
Smoked Bratwurst

Sausage Cont'd

Jennie-O Turkey Store ***
www.jennieo.com; 800-621-3505

Cheddar Turkey Bratwurst
Fully Cooked Lean Turkey Kielbasa
Fully Cooked Lean Turkey Sausage
Hot Lean Italian Turkey Style Sausage
Lean Turkey Bratwurst
Sweet Lean Italian Turkey Sausage

Johnsonville
www.johnsonville.com; 888-556-2728

Ground Sausage Hot, Mild and Sweet
Italian Sausage Four Cheese
Italian Sausage Hot, Mild and Sweet

Smithfield
www.smithfield.com

Hot Smoked Sausage Links
Smoked Sausage Loops
Smoked Sausage with Cheese

Perimeter:
Bakery

Breads

Gluten-free baked products, like bread, bagels, muffins, and pre-made pizza crusts, may be in your grocer's freezer aisle or in the "natural foods" aisle instead of the bakery.

Ener-G Foods
www.ener-g.com; 800-331-5222

> Brown English Muffins with Flax
> Brown Rice Hamburger Buns
> Brown Rice Loaf
> Egg-Free Raisin Loaf
> English Muffins
> Four Flour Loaf
> Hi Fiber Loaf
> Papas Loaf
> Seattle Brown Loaf
> Seattle Hamburger Buns
> Seattle Hot Dog Buns
> Tapioca Dinner Rolls
> Tapioca Hamburger Buns
> Tapioca Hot Dog Buns
> Tapioca Loaf
> White Rice Flax Loaf
> White Rice Hamburger Buns
> White Rice Loaf

Breads Cont'd

Rudi's Gluten Free Bakery *
www.rudisglutenfree.com; 877-293-0876

Sandwich
Multi Grain
Cinnamon Raisin

Schar
www.schar.com/us

Baguette
Bon Matin
Ciabattina Rustica
Ciabattine
Ertha
Foccacia
Foccacia con Rosmarino
Mini Baguette Duo
Pan Carre
Panini
Rustico

Breads Cont'd

Udi's Gluten Free Bakery ***
udisglutenfree.com; 303-657-6366

    Bagels
    Sandwich
    Multi Grain

Note

An alternative to buying bread is making it yourself. The Breadman TR875 and Zojirushi Home Bakery Supreme are bread-makers with gluten-free bread settings.

Making bread at home can be really easy with the boxed gluten-free bread mixes. I like the Gluten Free Pantry bread mixes and the King Arthur Flour Bread Mix.

However, making your own bread may not save money. Buying pre-made gluten-free bread costs between four and six dollars per loaf. Making bread from a boxed bread mix costs about the same; but, the homemade loaves weigh more.

Perimeter: Dairy

Milks

Plain milk, half and half, and whipping cream are naturally gluten-free. Be cautious of added flavoring.

Coffee-Mate
www.coffee-mate.com

All

Horizon
www.horizondairy.com; 888-494-3020

All

Nesquik
www.nesquik.com

All Ready-to-Drink flavors

Milks Cont'd

Organic Valley
www.organicvalley.coop; 888-444-6455

Buttermilk
Chocolate 2% Milk
Eggnog
Fat Free/Nonfat/Skim Milk
Half and Half
Heavy Whipping Cream
Lactose Free Milk
Lowfat 1% Milk
Omega-3 Milk
Reduced Fat 2% Milk
Single Serve Chocolate
Single Serve Lowfat
Single Serve Strawberry
Single Serve Vanilla
Soy Milk Chocolate
Soy Milk Original
Soy Milk Unsweetened
Soy Milk Vanilla
Whole Milk

Milks Cont'd

Pacific Natural Foods
www.pacificfoods.com; 503-924-4570

All Almond Beverages
All Hazelnut Beverages
All Hemp Beverages
All Rice Beverages
All Soy Beverages
Organic Fat-Free Milk
Organic Reduced Fat Milk

Stonyfield
www.stonyfield.com; 800-776-2697

All Milks

Sour Creams

Breakstone's
brands.kraftfoods.com/breakstones; 877-535-5666

All Sour Creams

Daisy Brand ***
www.daisybrand.com; 877-292-9830

All Sour Creams

Knudsen
www.rwknudsenfamily.com; 888-569-6993

All Sour Creams

Organic Valley
www.organicvalley.coop; 888-444-6455

Lowfat Sour Cream
Regular Sour Cream

Tillamook
www.tillamookcheese.com

All Sour Creams

Yogurts

Dannon
www.dannon.com; 877-326-6668

> DANNON Plain Activa
> DANNON Plain Yogurts (Lowfat, Nonfat, and Natural)

Stonyfield *
www.stonyfield.com; 800-776-2697

> All Fat Free Yogurt varieties
> All Low Fat B-Well Yogurt varieties
> All Low Fat Yogurt varieties
> All O'Soy varieties
> All Smoothie varieties
> All Whole Milk Yogurt varieties

Tillamook
www.tillamookcheese.com

> All

Perimeter:
Juices

Juices

Bolthouse Farms ***
www.bolthouse.com; 800-467-4683

All

Country Time Lemonade
brands.kraftfoods.com/countrytime; 877-535-5666

Bottles and cans

Dole
www.dole.com; 800-356-3111

All 100% Juices

Florida's Natural
www.floridasnatural.com; 888-657-6600

All

Kern's
www.kerns.com; 888-655-3767

All

Juices Cont'd

Knouse Foods
www.knouse.com; 717-677-8181

> Apple Cider
> Apple Juice
> Premium Apple Juice
> Sparkling Apple Cider

Minute Maid
www.minutemaid.com; 888-884-8952

> All Orange Juices and Blends
> Kids + Apple
> Kiwi-Strawberry Energy
> Lemonade–Regular and Light
> Pomegranate Blueberry
> Pomegranate Lemonade

Naked
www.nakedjuice.com; 877-858-4237

> All Fruit and Vegetable Juice products (with exceptions)
> **AVOID** Green Machine

Ocean Spray
www.oceanspray.com; 800-662-3263

> All

Odwalla
www.odwalla.com; 800-639-2552

All (with exceptions)
AVOID Super Protein Vanilla Al Mondo
AVOID Original Superfood

Organic Valley
www.organicvalley.coop; 888-444-6455

Orange Juice with Calcium
Orange Juice, Pulp-Added
Orange Juice, Pulp-Free

Simply Brand
www.simplyorangejuice.com; 800-871-2653

Apple
Grapefruit
Lemonade
Lemonade with Raspberry
Limeaide
Orange Juice
Orange with Mango
Orange with Pineapple

Juices Cont'd

Tree Top
www.treetop.com; 800-542-4055

All

Tropicana
www.tropicana.com; 800-237-7799

All Juice Drinks
All Pure Premium

V8
www.v8juice.com

All

Welch's
www.welchs.com; 800-340-6870

All

Perimeter: Cheeses

Cheeses

Applegate Farms
www.applegatefarms.com; 866-587-5858

Natural American
Natural Havarti
Natural New York Extra Sharp Aged Cheddar
Natural Cheddar–Medium
Natural Emmantaler Swiss
Natural Monterey Jack with Jalapeno Peppers
Natural Muenster Kase
Natural Provolone
Organic American
Organic Mild Cheddar
Organic Monterey Jack
Organic Muenster Kase
Organic Provolone
Probiotic Yogurt Cheese

Athenos
www.athenos.com; 877-535-5666

All

Breakstone's
brands.kraftfoods.com/breakstones; 877-535-5666

All Cottage Cheese products

Cheeses Cont'd

Frigo ***
www.frigocheese.com; 800-824-3373

> All Ricottas
> Blue Cheese
> Edam
> Feta
> Gouda
> Mozzarella
> Muenster
> Provolone
> Queso Rico

Knudsen
www.rwknudsenfamily.com; 888-569-6993

> All Cottage Cheese products

Kraft
www.kraftrecipes.com; 877-535-5666

> All Kraft Natural Cheese Sticks
> All Kraft Singles products

Laughing Cow ***
www.thelaughingcow.com; 800-272-1224

> All Babybel and Laughing Cow Wedges

Cheeses Cont'd

Organic Valley
www.organicvalley.coop; 888-444-6455

Baby Swiss
Cheddar Stringles
Colby
Colby-Jack Stringles
Cream Cheese
Feta
Mild Cheddar
Monterey Jack
Mozzarella
Mozzarella Stringles
Muenster
Neufchatel
Pepper Jack
Provolone
Raw Mild Cheddar
Raw Sharp Cheddar
Reduced Fat and Sodium Cheddar
Reduced Fat Monterey Jack
Ricotta
Sharp Cheddar
Shredded Italian Blend
Shredded Mexican Blend
Shredded Mild Cheddar
Shredded Parmesan
Shredded, Low Moisture, Part Skim Mozzarella

Cheeses Cont'd

Organic Valley Cont'd

Vermont Extra Sharp Cheddar
Vermont Medium Cheddar
Wisconsin Raw Milk Jack-Style

Philadelphia Cream Cheese
www.kraftbrands.com/philly; 877-535-5666

All cream cheeses
AVOID Bagel and Cream Cheese
AVOID Snack Bars
AVOID Snack Bites

Sargento
www.sargento.com; 800-243-3737

All Ricottas
All Shredded and Sliced varieties
AVOID Blue Cheese and MooTown Cheese
Dip Snack

Tillamook ***
www.tillamookcheese.com

All

Cheeses Cont'd

Velveeta
brands.kraftfoods.com/velveeta; 877-535-5666

    Cheese Slices
    Cheese Mexican Mild
    Cheese Regular

Aisles:
Beverages

Coffees

Ground and whole-bean coffee for use in your coffee maker is gluten-free.

Caribou Coffee
www.cariboucoffee.com; 888-227-4268

    All Iced Coffees

Pacific Natural Foods
www.pacificfoods.com; 503-924-4570

    All Simply Coffees

Starbucks
www.starbucks.com; 800-235-2883

    All bottled beverages

Drink Mixes

Coffee-Mate
www.coffee-mate.com

>   All Powders

Country Time Lemonade
brands.kraftfoods.com/countrytime; 877-535-5666

>   All Dry Mixes

Jose Cuervo
www.cuervo.com; 866-325-4990

>   Margarita Mix

Master of Mixes
www.masterofmixes.com; 800-474-3585

>   All regular mixes except Bloody Mary Mixes
>   **AVOID** Bloody Mary Mixes
>   All Big Bucket Mixes
>   All Cocktail Essentials
>   All Martini Gold

Drink Mixes Cont'd

Nesquik
www.nesquik.com

All Syrup flavors

On the Border
www.trucoenterprises.com; 800-471-7723

All Mixes

Swiss Miss
800-457-6649

Milk Chocolate Hot Cocoa Mix

Note

Making hot cocoa from scratch is easy. Before knowing there were gluten-free hot cocoa mixes, my wife would make it using unsweetened cocoa, sugar, milk, and vanilla. A hot cocoa recipe is on the side of most Hershey's Unsweetened Cocoa containers.

Flavored Waters

Aquafina
www.aquafina.com

   All

Aquafina Sparkling
www.aquafina.com

   All

Dasani
www.dasani.com; 800-438-2653

      Essence
      Lemon

Dasani Plus
www.dasani.com; 800-438-2653

      Cleanse+Restore
      Refresh+Revive

Fuze
www.drinkfuze.com; 800-208-2653

   All

Flavored Waters Cont'd

Owater
www.owater.com; 978-405-6300

Unsweetened Lemon & Lime
Unsweetened Mandarin Orange
Unsweetened Peach
Unsweetened Strawberry
Unsweetened Wild Berries

Propel
www.propelzero.com; 877-377-6735

All

Sobe Lifewater
www.sobe.com

All

Note

Create a short bulleted list of commonly available gluten-free drinks and snacks. Print it out for other parents, teachers, and coaches, and give it to them before parties, snack days, and holidays.

Ask that they please consider buying from your list so your child, who is on a gluten-free diet, may enjoy the same treats as everyone else.

Be sure to return the favor for friends who have allergies of their own. Companies like Enjoy Life make gluten-free products that are free of other top allergens, such as dairy, peanuts, and soy.

Kids' Drinks

Apple & Eve
www.appleandeve.com; 800-969-8018

   All

Capri Sun
brands.kraftfoods.com/caprisun; 877-535-5666

   All

Hansen's
www.hansens.com; 800-426-7367

   All

Welch's
www.welchs.com; 800-340-6870

   All

Sodas/Pops

7Up
www.7up.com; 800-696-5891

All

Barq's
www.barqs.com; 800-438-2653

Barq's Root Beer
Caffeine-Free Barq's Root Beer
Diet Barq's Red Crème Soda
Diet Barq's Root Beer

Club Soda

All varieties

Coke
www.coca-cola.com; 800-488-2267

Caffeine Free Coca-Cola Classic
Caffeine Free Diet Coke
Cherry Coke
Cherry Coke Zero
Coca-Cola Classic
Coca-Cola Zero
Diet Cherry Coke
Diet Coke

Aisles: Beverages

Coke Cont'd

Diet Coke Plus
Diet Coke Sweetened with Splenda
Diet Coke with Lime
Vanilla Coke
Vanilla Coke Zero

Dr. Pepper
www.drpepper.com; 800-696-5891

All

Fanta
www.coca-cola.com; 800-438-2653

Fanta Grape
Fanta Orange
Fanta Orange Zero

Fiesta Mirinda
www.pepsiproductfacts.com

All

Fresca
www.fresca.com; 800 438-2653

Fresca

Sodas/Pops Cont'd

Izze ***
www.izze.com; 303-327-5515

    All flavors

Kas Mas
www.pepsiproductfacts.com

    Kas Mas

Manzanita Sol
www.pepsiproductfacts.com

    Manzanita Sol

Mountain Dew
www.mountaindew.com

    All

Mug
www.mugrootbeer.com

    All

Sodas/Pops Cont'd

No Fear
www.pepsiproductfacts.com

   All

NOS
www.drinknos.com; 800-488-2267

   All

Pepsi
www.pepsi.com

   All

Sierra Mist
www.sierramist.com

   All

Slice
www.pepsiproductfacts.com

   All

Sodas/Pops Cont'd

Sobe
www.sobe.com

>All Sodas
>All Adrenalin Rush
>All Lean

Sprite
www.coca-cola.com; 800-488-2267

>Sprite
>Sprite Zero

Tonic Water

>All varieties

Tropicana Twister
www.tropicana.com; 800-237-7799

>All Tropicana Twister Sodas

Sport Drinks

G2
www.gatorade.com; 800-884-2867

All

Gatorade
www.gatorade.com; 800-884-2867

All

Owater
www.owater.com; 978-405-6300

Sport Black Razz
Sport Blueberry
Sport Coconut
Sport Lime Lemon
Sport Peach Mango
Sport Straw Pom
Sport Tropical Citrus

Powerade
www.us.powerade.com; 800-488-2267

All POWERADE with ION4
All POWERADE Zero with ION4

Sport Drinks Cont'd

VIO Vibrancy Drinks
www.viovibe.com

All

Note

Along with sport drinks, energy bars are often used to help replenish energy during or after exercise. Unfortunately, there are few gluten-free energy bars available and even fewer that taste good.

Consider making your own trail mix as an easy alternative. I buy cashews, peanuts, almonds, raisins, and chocolate chips, and mix them all together in a bag.

Substitute chocolate chips with M&M's on warm days to avoid melted chocolate chips and sticky hands!

Teas (Bags and Bottles)

Bigelow Tea
www.bigelowtea.com; 888-244-3569

    All Tea Bags

Celestial Seasonings
www.celestialseasonings.com; 866-595-8917

    All Tea Bags

Enviga
www.coca-cola.com; 800-438-2653

    Berry Sparkling Green Tea
    Sparkling Green Tea

Gold Peak
www.goldpeaktea.com; 800-438-2653

    All

Lipton
www.liptont.com; 888-547-8668

    All Iced Teas
    All Pureleaf
    All Sparkling
    All Lipton Tea Bags

Teas (Bags and Bottles) Cont'd

Luzianne
www.luzianne.com; 800-535-1961

 All Tea Bags

Minute Maid
www.minutemaid.com; 888-884-8952

 Pomegranate Flavored Tea

Nestea
www.nestea.com; 800-488-2267

 Citrus Green Tea
 Diet Citrus Green Tea
 Diet Lemon
 Lemon Sweet Tea
 Red Tea
 Sweetened Lemon Tea

Aisles:
Baking

Baking-Related

Argo
www.argostarch.com; 866-373-2300

Baking Powder
Corn Starch

Arm & Hammer
www.armhammer.com; 800-524-1328

Baking Soda

Betty Crocker ***
www.bettycrocker.com; 800-446-1898

Gluten Free Brownie Mix
Gluten Free Cake Mix
Gluten Free Cookie Mix

Bisquick
www.bettycrocker.com/products/bisquick/; 800-446-1898

Gluten Free Pancake and Baking Mix

Baking-Related Cont'd

Bob's Red Mill
www.bobsredmill.com; 800-349-2173

Baking Soda
Corn Starch
GF Biscuit Mix
GF Brownie Mix
GF Chocolate Cake Mix
GF Chocolate Chip Cookie Mix
GF Cinnamon Raisin Bread Mix
GF Cornbread Mix
GF Hearty Whole Grain Bread
GF Homemade Wonderful Bread
GF Pancake Mix
GF Pizza Crust Mix
GF Shortbread Cookie Mix
GF Vanilla Cake Mix

Calumet
www.kraftrecipes.com; 877-535-5666

Baking Powder

Clabber Girl
www.clabbergirl.com; 812-232-9446

Baking Powder

Baking-Related Cont'd

Diamond Nuts
www.diamondnuts.com; 209 467-6000

All Diamond-branded nut products

Ener-G Foods
www.ener-g.com; 800-331-5222

Brown Rice Flour
Corn Mix
Gluten-Free Gourmet Blend
Potato Flour
Potato Mix
Potato Starch Flour
Rice Mix
Sweet Rice Flour
Tapioca Flour
White Rice Flour

Ghirardelli Chocolate Company
www.ghirardelli.com; 800-877-9338

60% Cacao Bittersweet Chocolate Chip
Barista Dark Chocolate Chip
Semi-Sweet Chocolate Chip
Unsweetened Cocoa Powder

Baking-Related Cont'd

Guittard
www.guittard.com; 800-468-2462

    Cocoa Rouge Unsweetened Cocoa Powder

Fleischmann's Yeast
www.breadworld.com; 800-777-4959

    All Yeasts

Hershey's
www.hersheys.com; 800 468-1714

    Unsweetened Cocoa

King Arthur Flour Company *
www.kingarthurflour.com; 800-827-6836

    Gluten-Free All Purpose Flour
    Gluten-Free Bread Mix
    Gluten-Free Brownie Mix
    Gluten-Free Cake Mix
    Gluten-Free Cookie Mix
    Gluten-Free Muffin Mix
    Gluten-Free Pancake Mix

Baking-Related Cont'd

Mary's Gone Crackers
www.marysgonecrackers.com; 888-258-1250

Gone Crackers Crumbs Caraway
Gone Crackers Crumbs Original
Gone Crackers Crumbs Savory Blend

Mazola
www.mazola.com; 800-691-1106

All Oils

McCormick & Company, Inc.
www.mccormick.com; 800-632-5847

All Extracts

Pamela's *
www.pamelasproducts.com; 707-462-6605

Baking & Pancake Mix
Chocolate Brownie Mix
Chocolate Cake Mix
Chocolate Chunk Cookies
Classic Vanilla Cake Mix
Cornbread & Muffin Mix
Gluten-Free Bread Mix

Baking-Related Cont'd

Red Star Yeast
www.redstaryeast.com; 800-445-4746

　　All Yeasts

Simply Organic
www.simplyorganicfoods.com; 800-437-3301

　　Almond Extract
　　Banana Bread Mix
　　Carrot Cake Mix
　　Chai Spice Scone Mix
　　Cocoa Biscotti Mix
　　Cocoa Brownie Mix
　　Cocoa Cayenne Cupcake Mix
　　Lemon, Orange, Peppermint Flavor
　　Pancake & Waffle Mix
　　Vanilla Extract

Spice Islands
www.spiceislands.com; 800-247-5251

　　All Liquid Extracts, Flavorings, and Colorings

Tone's
www.tones.com; 800-247-5251

　　All Liquid Extracts, Flavorings, and Colorings

Canned Milks

Carnation
www.verybestbaking.com/Carnation.aspx; 800-851-0512

Evaporated Milk

Eagle Brand
www.eaglebrand.com; 888-656-3245

All Condensed Milks

Nestle
www.nestle.com; 818-549-6000

Sweetened Condensed Milk

Santini Foods
www.santinifoods.com; 510-317-8888

All Milks

Frostings

Betty Crocker
www.bettycrocker.com; 800-446-1898

All

Duncan Hines
www.duncanhines.com; 800-362-9834

All

Gelatins

Jell-O
brands.kraftfoods.com/jello; 877-535-5666

> All Gelatin Desserts
> All Gelatin Snacks

Pie Fillings

Knouse Foods
www.knouse.com; 717-677-8181

    Apple
    Apricot
    Banana Crème
    Blackberry
    Blueberry
    Cherries Jubilee
    Cherry
    Chocolate Crème
    Coconut Crème
    Dark Sweet Cherry
    Key Lime
    Lemon
    Lemon Crème
    Lite Apple
    Lite Cherry
    Peach
    Pineapple
    Raisin
    Strawberry
    Strawberry Glaze
    Vanilla Crème

Pie Fillings Cont'd

Libby's
www.verybestbaking.com/Libbys.aspx; 800-854-0374

Pumpkin Pie Filling
Solid Pack Pumpkin

Wilderness
www.piefilling.com

All Pie Fillings

Note

Making your own gluten-free pie crust is relatively easy and a much cheaper alternative than buying one! However, gluten-free dough is often difficult to work with.

For pie crusts, my wife rolls the finished dough in a ball, puts it directly into the pie pan, covers it with a piece of plastic wrap, and then pushes it into a crust in the pan.

Aisles:
Canned Foods

Beans

B&M Baked Beans
www.bgfoods.com/bm/bm_index.asp?n=3

All varieties

Bush's Best
www.bushbeans.com

All canned after May 2010

Casa Fiesta
www.casafiesta.com; 800-299-9082

Refried Beans

Fantastic World Foods
www.fantasticfoods.com

Instant Black Beans
Instant Refried Beans

Beans Cont'd

Hanover Foods Corporation
www.hanoverfoods.com; 717-632-6000

Beans & Franks
Black Beans
Blackeye Peas
Brown Sugar & Bacon Baked Beans
Butter Beans
Chick Peas
Chili Beans
Great Northern Beans
Homestyle Baked Beans
Limagrands
Pinto Beans
Pork & Beans
Red Beans
Redskin Kidney Beans (Light & Dark)
Seasoned Black Beans

Joan of Arc
www.bgfoods.com

Black Beans
Butter Beans
Garbanzo Beans

Beans Cont'd

Joan of Arc Cont'd

Red Beans
Great Northern Beans
Light & Dark Red Kidney Beans
Pinto Beans

Kid's Kitchen
www.hormel.com; 800-523-4635

Beans & Wieners

Kuner's

Black Beans
Pinto Beans

Ortega
www.ortega.com

Refried Regular & Fat Free Beans
Black Beans
Black Beans with Jalapenos

Rosarita ***
800-365-8300

Refried Beans

Chili's and Stews

Cookwell & Company
www.cookwell.net; 512-306-0044

      Two-Step Cacciatore
      Two-Step Chili
      Two-Step Green Chili Stew
      Two-Step Veracruz

Dinty Moore
www.hormelfoods.com; 800-523-4635

      Beef Stew
      Chicken Stew
      Beef Stew (Microwaveable Cups)
      Rice with Chicken (Microwaveable Cups)
      Scalloped Potatoes & Ham (Microwaveable Cups)

Chili's and Stews Cont'd

Hormel
www.hormelfoods.com; 800-523-4635

Bean & Ham Soup (Microwaveable Cups)
Chicken with Vegetables & Rice Soup
(Microwaveable Cups)
Chili Master–Chipotle Chicken No Bean
Chili Master–Chipotle Chicken with Beans
White Chicken Chili with Beans
Chili with Beans-Chunky
Chili with Beans-Hot–Not Vegetarian
Chili with Beans-Not Turkey
Chili with Beans-Regular

Stagg
www.staggchili.com; 800-611-9778

Chunkero Chili
Classic Chili
Dynamite Hot Chili
Ranch House Chicken Chili
Silverado Beef Chili
Steak House Chili
Vegetable Garden Chili
White Chicken Chili

Fruits and Vegetables

B&G
www.bgfoods.com

> Capers
> Green & Black Olives
> Pickles

Del Monte
www.delmonte.com; 800-543-3090

> All canned and jarred fruit
> All canned vegetables

Dole
www.dole.com; 800-356-3111

> All canned fruit
> All dried fruit
> All Fruit Bowls and Fruit in Jars

S&W
www.delmonte.com; 800-543-3090

> All canned fruits
> All canned vegetables

Peppers

B&G
www.bgfoods.com

All peppers

Embasa
www.hormelfoods.com; 800-523-4635

Chiles Gueritos
Chipotle Peppers
Nacho Sliced Jalapenos
Sliced Jalapenos
Whole Jalapenos

La Victoria
www.lavictoria.com; 800-523-4635

All peppers

Las Palmas
www.bgfoods.com

Crushed Tomatillos

Peppers Cont'd

Ortega
www.ortega.com

> Chilies
> Jalapenos

Rosarita
800-365-8300

> All peppers

Soups

Amy's
www.amys.com; 707-568-4500

Black Bean and Vegetable
Curried Lentil Soup
Hearty French Country Vegetable
Hearty Rustic Italian Vegetable
Hearty Spanish Rice & Red Bean
Indian Dal Golden Lentil
Organic Chunky Tomato Bisque
Organic Chunky Tomato Bisque–Light in Sodium
Organic Chunky Vegetable
Organic Cream of Tomato
Organic Cream of Tomato–Light in Sodium
Organic Fire Roasted Southwestern Vegetable
Organic Lentil
Organic Lentil–Light in Sodium
Organic Lentil Vegetable
Organic Lentil Vegetable–Light in Sodium
Organic Split Pea
Organic Split Pea–Light in Vegetable
Organic Tuscan Bean & Rice
Summer Corn & Vegetable
Thai Coconut

Soups Cont'd

Fantastic World Foods
www.fantasticfoods.com

Blarneystone Creamy Potato Soup Mix
Cha Cha Chili Bean Soup Mix
Dutch Split Pea Soup Mix

Imagine Natural Creations *
www.imaginefoods.com; 800-434-4246

Beef Flavored Broth
Beef Flavored Broth Low Sodium
Beef Flavored Cooking Stock Low Sodium
Chicken Cooking Stock
Chicken Cooking Stock Low Sodium
Creamy Acorn Squash & Mango Soup
Creamy Broccoli Soup
Creamy Butternut Squash Soup
Creamy Corn & Lemongrass Soup
Creamy Garden Broccoli Soup
Creamy Garden Tomato Soup
Creamy Harvest Corn Soup
Creamy Portobello Mushroom Soup
Creamy Potato Leek Soup
Creamy Red Bliss Potato & Roasted Garlic Soup
Creamy Sweet Pea Soup

Soups Cont'd

Imagine Natural Creations Cont'd

Creamy Sweet Potato Soup
Creamy Sweet Potato Soup Light in Sodium
Creamy Tomato Basil Soup
Creamy Tomato Soup
Free Range Chicken Broth
Free Range Chicken Broth Low Sodium
No-Chicken Broth
Roasted Turkey Gravy
Savory Beef Gravy
Vegetable Broth
Vegetable Broth Low Sodium
Vegetable Cooking Stock

Kettle Cuisine ***
www.kettlecuisine.com; 877-302-SOUP

All soups

Pacific Natural Foods ***
www.pacificfoods.com; 503-924-4570

Buttery Sweet Corn
Cashew Carrot Ginger
Creamy Roasted Carrot
Curried Red Lentil
Natural Beef Broth

Soups Cont'd

Pacific Natural Foods Cont'd

Natural Free Range Chicken Broth
Organic Beef Broth
Organic Creamy Butternut Squash
Organic Creamy RRP & Tomato
Organic Creamy Tomato
Organic Free Range Chicken Broth
Organic French Onion
Organic Light Sodium Butternut Squash
Organic Light Sodium Creamy Tomato
Organic Light Sodium RRP & Tomato
Organic Low Sodium Chicken Broth
Organic Low Sodium Vegetable Broth
Organic Mushroom Broth
Organic Savory Chicken & Wild Rice
Organic Savory White Bean with Bacon
Organic Spicy Black Bean with Chicken Sausage
Organic Spicy Chicken Fajita
Organic Split Pea with Ham & Swiss Cheese
Organic Vegetable Broth
Spicy Black Bean Soup
Tuscan White Bean Soup

Aisles: Canned Foods

Progresso
www.progressofoods.com; 800-200-9377

Traditional 99% Fat Free New England Clam Chowder
Traditional Chicken Cheese Enchilada Flavor
Traditional Chicken Rice with Vegetables
Traditional Manhattan Clam Chowder
Traditional New England Clam Chowder
Traditional Potato, Broccoli & Cheese Chowder
Traditional Southwestern-Style Chicken
Traditional Split Pea with Ham
Vegetable Classics 99% Fat Free Lentil
Vegetable Classics Creamy Mushroom
Vegetable Classics Lentil

Right Foods
www.rightfoods.com; 800-367-3844

Black Bean & Lime Soup Cup
Black Bean Soup
Chunky Tomato Soup
Lentil
Light Sodium Split Pea Soup Cup

Soups Cont'd

Right Foods Cont'd

Pad Thai Noodle Soup Cup
Roasted Pepper Tomato Soup
Spring Onion Noodle Soup Cup
Tamale Soup Cup
Tortilla Soup Cup
Vegetable Soup

Swanson
www.swansonbroth.com; 800-442-7684

Chicken Broth (canned)
Natural Goodness Chicken Broth (canned)
Vegetable Broth (canned)

Note

Pay careful attention when choosing your soup. Many soups contain gluten. Not all soups made by a *company* listed in this soup section are gluten-free. Only specific products listed here are known to be gluten-free at publication.

Tomato-Related

Dei Fratelli
www.deifratelli.com; 800-837-1631

All

Del Monte
www.delmonte.com; 800-543-3090

All

Aisles:

Dessert-Related

Puddings

Jell-O
brands.kraftfoods.com/jello; 877-535-5666

Cheesecake Snacks
Mousse Temptations
Pudding & Pie Filling Cook & Server
Pudding & Pie Filling Instant
Pudding Snacks

Kozy Shack ***
www.kozyshack.com

All Puddings, Flans, and Gels

Note

Dry pudding mixes aren't just for pudding! Anne Byrn's *The Cake Mix Doctor Bakes Gluten-Free* has several cake and muffin recipes where you mix dry pudding with cake mix. My wife made a birthday cake using one of her recipes and it was a hit.

Toppings

Cool Whip
brands.kraftfoods.com/coolwhip; 877-535-5666

All

Smucker's
www.smuckers.com; 888-550-9555

Magic Shell Caramel
Magic Shell Cherry
Magic Shell Chocolate
Magic Shell Chocolate Fudge
Magic Shell Cupcake
Magic Shell Orange Crème
Microwave Toppings Hot Fudge
Special Recipe Butterscotch Caramel
Special Recipe Dark Chocolate
Special Recipe Hot Fudge
Special Recipe Triple Berry
Toppings Apple Cinnamon
Toppings Black Cherry
Toppings Butterscotch
Toppings Caramel
Toppings Chocolate Fudge
Toppings Hot Caramel
Toppings Hot Fudge
Toppings Marshmallow
Toppings Pecans in Syrup

Toppings Cont'd

Smucker's Cont'd

Toppings Pineapple
Toppings Pumpkin Spice
Toppings Strawberry
Toppings Walnuts in Syrup

Aisles:

Dry Goods

Cereals

Barbara's
www.barbarasbakery.com; 800-343-0590 x1032

Brown Rice Crisps
Honey Rice Puffins
Multigrain Puffins

Bob's Red Mill
www.bobsredmill.com; 800-349-2173

Creamy Brown Rice Farina
GF Mighty Tasty Hot Cereal

Eco-Planet
www.ecoheavenllc.com; 630-701-8801

Instant Hot Cereal Apples & Cinnamon
Instant Hot Cereal Maple & Brown Sugar
Instant Hot Cereal Original

General Mills ***
www.generalmills.com; 800-248-7310

Chocolate Chex
Cinnamon Chex
Corn Chex
Honey Nut Chex
Rice Chex

Cereals Cont'd

Nature's Path ***
www.naturespath.com; 888-808-9505

Amazon Frosted Flakes
Crispy Rice Cereal
Crunchy Maple Surprise
Crunchy Vanilla Surprise
Fruit Juice Sweetened Corn Flakes
Gorilla Munch
Honey'd Corn Flakes
Koala Crisp
Leapin' Lemurs
Mesa Sunrise
Panda Puffs
Whole O's Cereal

Note

Kellogg's Rice Krispies are not gluten-free nor are pre-made Rice Krispies Treats. Most marshmallows are gluten-free so make your own treats using gluten-free rice crisp cereals. My kids like chocolate rice crisp treats made using Nature's Path Koala Crisp cereal.

I've read that Kellogg's is coming out with gluten-free Rice Krispies Treats soon, so stay tuned.

Pastas

Annie's ***
www.annies.com; 800 288-1089

> Gluten Free Delux Rice Pasta and Extra Creamy Cheddar
> Gluten Free Rice Pasta and Cheddar

DeBoles
www.deboles.com; 800-434-4246

> Gluten Free Angel Hair
> Gluten Free Corn Elbow Style
> Gluten Free Multi Grain Penne
> Gluten Free Multi Grain Spaghetti Style
> Gluten Free Rice Lasagna
> Gluten Free Rice Pasta & Cheese
> Gluten Free Rice Shells & Cheddar
> Gluten Free Rice Spirals
> Gluten Free Spaghetti

Ener-G Foods
www.ener-g.com; 800-331-5222

> White Rice Lasagna
> White Rice Macaroni
> White Rice Pasta
> White Rice Small Shells
> White Rice Vermicelli

Pastas Cont'd

Glutino
www.glutino.com; 800-363-3438

   All

Schar
www.schar.com/us

   Angellini
   Capelli d'Angelo
   Conchigliette
   Fusilli
   Lasagna
   Penne
   Pipette
   Rigati
   Rigatoni
   Spaghetti
   Tagliatelle

Thai Kitchen
www.thaikitchen.com; 800-967-8424

   Stir-Fry Rice Noodles
   Thin Rice Noodles

Aisles: Dry Goods

Tinkyada ***
www.tinkyada.com; 416-609-0016

All

Note

Gluten-free pasta tastes better if you rinse it thoroughly.
Rinse the pasta with hot water when you strain it.

I also like to add a few drops of olive oil to the pasta
after rinsing it. The oil keeps the pasta from sticking
together. This is especially useful if you will be saving
some of the pasta as leftovers.

Pizza Crusts

Chebe Bread
www.chebe.com; 800-217-9510

    Gluten Free Pizza Crust

Ener-G Foods
www.ener-g.com; 800-331-5222

    Rice Pizza Shells
    Yeast-Free Rice Pizza Shells

Kinnikinnick Foods
consumer.kinnikinnick.com; 877-503-4466

    Gluten Free Pizza Crust

Udi's Gluten Free Bakery
udisglutenfree.com; 303-657-6366

    Gluten Free Pizza Crust

Whole Foods
www.wholefoodsmarket.com

    Bakehouse Gluten Free

Sides

Betty Crocker
www.bettycrocker.com; 800-446-1898

Asian Helper Beef Fried Rice
Asian Helper Chicken Fried Rice
Hamburger Helper Cheesy Hashbrowns
Potato Buds

Carolina Rice
www.carolinarice.com; 800-226-9522

Authentic Spanish Rice
Basmati Rice
Broccoli Cheese Rice
Brown Rice
Gold (Parboiled) Rice
Jasmine Rice
Long Grain & Wild Rice
Saffron Yellow Rice
White Rice

Sides Cont'd

Fantastic World Foods
www.fantasticfoods.com

> Arborio Rice
> Basmati Rice
> Jasmine Rice

Gourmet House Rice
www.gourmethouserice.com; 800-226-9522

> All Natural Brown and Wild Rice
> All Natural White and Wild Rice
> Brown Rice
> Cracked Minnesota Cultivated Wild Rice
> Organic Brown Rice
> Organic White Rice
> Quick-Cooking Wild Rice
> Thai Jasmine Rice
> White Rice
> Wild Rice Garden Blend

Idahoan
www.idahoan.com; 208-754-8046

> Baby Reds
> Baby Reds Garlic & Parm
> Butter & Herb
> Buttery Gold Selects

Sides Cont'd

Idahoan Cont'd
www.idahoan.com; 208-754-8046

Creamy Home Style
Earth Baby Reds
Buttery Home Style
Earth Buttery Home Style
Earth Creamy Mashed
Earth Yukon Golds
Four Cheese
Original Flakes
Real
Roasted Garlic
Romano White Cheese
Scalloped CN
Southwest
Yukon Golds

Lundberg Family Farms ***
www.lundberg.com; 530-882-4551

Butternut Squash Risotto
Cheddar Broccoli Risotto
Creamy Parmesan Risotto
Garlic Primavera Risotto
Italian Herb Risotto
Organic Alfredo Risotto

Sides Cont'd

Lundberg Family Farms Cont'd

Organic Florentine Risotto
Organic Porcini Mushroom Risotto
Organic Tuscan Risotto

Mahatma
www.mahatmarice.com; 800-226-9522

Authentic Spanish Rice
Basmati Rice
Black Beans and Rice
Broccoli Cheese Rice
Chicken Rice
Classic Pilaf Rice
Gold (Parboiled) Rice
Jasmine Rice
Long Grain & Wild Rice
Red Beans & Rice
Spicy Yellow Rice
White Rice
Whole Grain Brown Rice
Yellow Rice

Sides Cont'd

Minute Rice
www.minuterice.com; 800-646-8831

Brown Rice
MINUTE Ready to Serve Brown & Wild Rice
MINUTE Ready to Serve Brown Rice
MINUTE Ready to Serve Chicken Rice Mix
MINUTE Ready to Serve White Rice
MINUTE Ready to Serve Yellow Rice Mix
Premium White Rice
White Rice

Success Rice
www.successrice.com; 800-226-9522

Success Brown Rice
Success Jasmine Rice
Success White Rice

Tasty Bite
www.tastybite.com; 888-827-8900

Agra Peas & Greens
Aloo Palak
Basmati Rice
Bengal Lentils
Bombay Potatoes
Brown Rice
Channa Masala

Sides Cont'd

Tasty Bite Cont'd

Chunky Chickpeas
Garlic Brown Rice
Ginger Lentil Rice
Good Korma Simmer Sauce
Jaipur Vegetables
Jasmine Rice
Jodphur Lentils
Kashmir Spinach
Kerala Vegetables
Lentil Magic
Long Grain Rice
Madras Lentils
Mexican Fiesta Pilaf
Mushroom Takatak
Pad Thai Simmer Sauce
Paneer Makhani
Peas Paneer
Punjab Eggplant
Rogan Josh Simmer Sauce
Satay Partay Simmer Sauce
Snappy Soya

Sides Cont'd

Tasty Bite Cont'd

Spinach Dal
Tandoori Pilaf
Tehari Herb Rice
Tikka Masala Simmer Sauce
Vegetable Korma
Zany Multigrain
Zesty Lentils & Peas

Spices

Durkee
www.durkee.com; 800-247-5251

>All single-ingredient spices
>All California Style Blends

McCormick & Company, Inc.
www.mccormick.com; 800-632-5847

>Enchilada Sauce Mix
>Gourmet Collection single-ingredient spices and herbs
>Original Taco Seasoning
>Single-ingredient spices and herbs

Spice Islands
www.spiceislands.com; 800-247-5251

>All single-ingredient spices
>All Salt Free varieties
>All Grilling Gourmet varieties
>All World Flavors varieties
>Specialty Beau Monde
>Specialty Chili Powder
>Specialty Fine Herbs
>Specialty Crystallized Ginger
>Specialty Italian Herb Seasoning

Spices Cont'd

Spice Islands Cont'd

Specialty Garlic Pepper Seasoning
Specialty Saffron
Specialty Old Hickory Smoked Salt
Specialty Summer Savory
Specialty Vanilla Bean

Tone's
www.tones.com; 800-247-5251

All single-ingredient spices

Tortillas

Mission Foods Corporation ***
www.missionfoods.com

Corn Tortillas–Soft, Hard, White, or Yellow Corn

Ortega
www.ortega.com

Corn Tortillas–White or Yellow Corn
Hard Shells–Yellow & White Corn
Tostada Shells
Whole Grain

Note

Unfortunately, I have not found a suitable gluten-free replacement for the flour tortilla.

My wife and I have replaced traditional flour-wrapped burritos with burrito bowls (where the ingredients of the burrito are served in a bowl), tacos with corn shells, and casseroles.

Aisles:

Frozen Foods

Fruits and Vegetables

Bird's Eye C&W
www.birdseyefoods.com

Plain frozen vegetables (no sauces)

Dole
www.dole.com; 800-356-3111

All frozen fruits

Green Giant
www.bettycrocker.com/products/green-giant/; 800-446-1898

Plain frozen vegetables (no sauces)

Fruits and Vegetables Cont'd

Hanover Foods Corporation
www.hanoverfoods.com; 717-632-6000

Asparagus Spears
Baby Lima Beans
Blue Lake Cut Green Beans
Blue Lake French Green Beans
Blue Lake Whole Green Beans
Broccoli & Cauliflower Blend
Broccoli Cuts
Broccoli Florets (and Petites)
Brussel Sprouts Petite
California Blend
Carrots Sliced
Carrots Whole Baby
Cauliflower Clusters
Peas Petite
Snow Peas
Spinach Cut Leaf
Sugar Snap Peas
White Sweet Corn

Ice Creams

Breyers
www.icecreamusa.com; 800-931-2826

    Chocolate
    Chocolate Chip
    French Vanilla
    Mint Chocolate Chip
    Natural Vanilla
    Rocky Road
    Vanilla, Chocolate, Strawberry

Dreyer's
www.dreyers.com; 877-437-3937

    Grand Chocolate
    Grand Chocolate Chip
    Grand Neapolitan
    Grand Rocky Road
    Grand Vanilla

Mars
www.mars.com; 800-627-7852

    Snickers Regular and Mini Ice Cream Bars

Ice Creams Cont'd

Popsicle
www.popsicle.com; 800-931-2849

Orange Cherry Grape
Sugar Free Orange Cherry Grape

Note

As a general rule, avoid ice creams that have cookies or cookie dough as an ingredient.

Check out the "Aisles: Dessert-Related" section in this guide for a selection of ice cream toppings!

Meals

Amy's ***
www.amys.com; 707-568-4500

> Cheese Enchilada
> Garden Vegetable Lasagna
> Light & Lean Black Bean & Cheese Enchilada
> Light in Sodium Black Bean Enchilada
> Rice Mac & Cheese
> Vegan Rice Macaroni & Cheeze

Glutino
www.glutino.com; 800-363-3438

> BBQ Chicken Pizza
> Chicken Pad Thai
> Chicken Penne Alfredo
> Chicken Pomodoro
> Chicken Ranchero
> Duo Cheese Pizza
> Macaroni 'N Cheese
> Penne Alfredo
> Pepperoni Pizza
> Spinach & Feta Pizza
> Spinach Soy Cheese Pizza with Brown Rice Crust
> Three Cheese Pizza with Brown Rice Crust

Meals Cont'd

Ians
www.iansnaturalfoods.com; 800-543-6637

Gluten Free Chicken Finger Kids Meal
Gluten Free Egg & Maple Cheddar Wafflewiches
Gluten Free French Bread Pizza
Gluten Free French Toast Sticks
Gluten Free Lightly Battered Fish
Gluten Free Maple Sausage & Egg Wafflewiches
Gluten Free Popcorn Turkey Corn Dogs

Chicken

Applegate Farms ***
www.applegatefarms.com; 866-587-5858

   Natural Gluten Free Chicken Nuggets

Bell & Evans
www.bellandevans.com; 717-865-6626

   Gluten Free Breaded Chicken Breasts
   Gluten Free Breaded Chicken Patties
   Gluten Free Chicken Nuggets
   Gluten Free Chicken Tenders
   Gluten Free Garlic Parmesan Breaded Chicken
   Breasts
   Gluten Free Italian Style Breaded Chicken Patties

Ians
www.iansnaturalfoods.com; 800-543-6637

   Gluten Free Chicken Nuggets
   Gluten Free Chicken Patties
   Gluten Free Fish Sticks

Chicken Cont'd

Wellshire Farms ***
www.wellshirefarms.com; 877-467-2331

Kids' Chicken Bites Dinosaur Shaped

Note

Celiac disease may be genetic; therefore, it is a good idea for first-degree relatives to be tested. Ask your doctor about being screened for celiac disease and be sure to let them know if others in your family have been diagnosed.

Aisles: Infant/Toddler Foods

Infant/Toddler Foods

Earth's Best Organic
www.earthsbest.com; 800-434-4246

First Apples
First Bananas
First Carrots
First Pears
First Peas
First Prunes
First Squash
First Sweet Potatoes
2nd Fruits-Apples
2nd Fruits-Apples &Apricots
2nd Fruits-Apples & Bananas
2nd Fruits-Apples & Blueberries
2nd Fruits-Apples & Plums
2nd Fruits-Bananas
2nd Fruits-Bananas, Peaches & Raspberries
2nd Fruits-Pears
2nd Fruits-Pears & Mangos
2nd Fruits-Pears & Raspberries
2nd Vegetables-Carrots
2nd Vegetables-Corn & Butternut Squash
2nd Vegetables-Garden Vegetables
2nd Vegetables-Green Beans & Rice

Infant/Toddler Foods Cont'd

Earth's Best Organic Cont'd

2nd Vegetables-Peas & Brown Rice
2nd Vegetables-Sweet Potatoes
2nd Vegetables-Winter Squash
Infant Formula with Iron
Organic Grain Rice Cereal
Organic Whole Grain Rice Cereal
Organic Whole Grain Rice Cereal with Apples
Soy Infant Formula with Iron

Gerber
www.gerber.com; 800-284-9488

Graduates Lil' Crunchies-Garden Tomato
Graduates Lil' Crunchies-Mild Cheddar
Graduates Lil' Crunchies-Veggie Dip
Graduates Wagon Wheels-Apple Harvest
Graduates Wagon Wheels-Cheesy Carrot
Graduates Yogurt Melts-Mixed Berries
Graduates Yogurt Melts-Peach
Graduates Yogurt Melts-Strawberry
Nature Select 1st Foods Fruits-Apples
Nature Select 1st Foods Fruits-Bananas
Nature Select 1st Foods Fruits-Peaches
Nature Select 1st Foods Fruits-Pears
Nature Select 1st Foods Fruits-Prunes

Infant/Toddler Foods Cont'd

Gerber Cont'd

Nature Select 1st Foods Vegetables-Carrots
Nature Select 1st Foods Vegetables-Peas
Nature Select 1st Foods Vegetables-Squash
Nature Select 1st Foods Vegetables-Sweet Potatoes
Nature Select 1st Foods Vegetables-Green Beans
Organic 1st Foods Fruits-Apples
Organic 1st Foods Fruits-Bananas
Organic 1st Foods Fruits-Pears
Organic 1st Foods Fruits-Prunes
Organic 1st Foods Vegetables-Carrots
Organic 1st Foods Vegetables-Sweet Peas
Organic 1st Foods Vegetables-Sweet Potatoes

Happy Baby
www.happybabyfood.com; 212-374-2779

Frozen Meals-Baby Dahl & Mama Grain
Frozen Meals-Chick Chick
Frozen Meals-Easy Going Greens & Great Greens
Frozen Meals-Gobble Gobble & Paradise Puree
Frozen Meals-Sweeter Potatoes & Purer Pears
Frozen Meals-Yes Peas and Thank You Carrots
Happybellies Cereal-Brown Rice
Melts-Organic Banana Mango
Melts-Organic Mixed Berry
Melts-Organic Strawberry

Infant/Toddler Foods Cont'd

Happy Baby Cont'd

Pouches-Amaranth Ratatouille
Pouches-Apple & Cherry
Pouches-Apricot & Sweet Potato
Pouches-Banana, Beet & Blueberry
Pouches-Beef Stew
Pouches-Broccoli, Pear & Peas
Pouches-Chick Chick
Pouches-Gobble Gobble
Pouches-Kiwi & Banana
Pouches-Mama Grain
Pouches-Mango
Pouches-Pear
Pouches-Spinach, Mango & Pear
Pouches-Super Salmon
Puffs-GF Strawberry
Puffs-GF Sweet Potato
Tots-Apple & Butternut Squash
Tots-Banana, Mango & Peach
Tots-Banana, Peach, Prunes & Coconut
Tots-Green Beans, Pears & Peas
Tots-Spinach, Mango & Pear
Tots-Sweet Potato, Apple, Carrots & Cinnamon

Mum Mum
www.mummums.com; 888-894-6464

All Baby and Toddler Mum Mum's

Infant/Toddler Foods Cont'd

Stonyfield
www.stonyfield.com; 800-776-2697

Yo Baby Drinkable Banana
Yo Baby Drinkable Peach
Yo Baby Meal Apple & Sweet Potato
Yo Baby Meal Peach & Squash
Yo Baby Meal Pear & Green Beans
Yo Baby Original Banana
Yo Baby Original Blueberry
Yo Baby Original Peach
Yo Baby Original Simply Plain
Yo Baby Original Vanilla

Aisles:

Oils, Sauces, and Spreads

Asian Sauces

Eden Organic *
www.edenfoods.com; 888 424-3336

Tamari Soy Sauce

Gold's Pure Food Products Co., Inc.
goldshorseradish.com; 516-483-5600

Hot & Spicy Duck Sauce
Oriental Garlic Duck Sauce
Squeeze Wasabi Sauce
Sweet & Sour Duck Sauce

San-J *
www.san-j.com; 800-446-5500

Asian BBQ Sauce
Organic Gluten Free Tamari Soy Sauce
Organic Reduced Sodium Gluten Free Tamari Soy
Sauce
Sweet & Tangy Sauce
Szechuan Sauce
Tamari Ginger Dressing
Tamari Peanut Dressing
Tamari Sesame Dressing
Teriyaki Sauce
Thai Peanut Sauce

Asian Sauces Cont'd

Thai Kitchen
www.thaikitchen.com; 800-967-8424

- Fish Sauce
- Original Pad Thai
- Peanut Satay
- Spicy Thai Chili
- Sweet Red Chili

Note

Did you know that most soy sauces contain wheat? Tamari soy sauce is an excellent replacement.

Barbecue Sauces

A-1
brands.kraftfoods.com/a1; 877-535-5666

Chicago Steakhouse
Jamaican Jerk
Steak Sauce
Steak Sauce Smokey Mesquite
Steak Sauce Supreme Garlic
Steak Sauce Teriyaki
Steak Sauce Thick & Hearty
Texas Mesquite

Bill Johnson's
billjohnsonsbbqsauce.com; 602-477-0790

All

Frank's Red Hot
www.franksredhot.com; 800-841-1256

Chile 'n Lime Sauce

Barbecue Sauces Cont'd

Heinz
www.heinz.com; 800-255-5750

Barbecue Sauce
BBQ Sauce Honey Garlic
Chicken & Rib BBQ Sauce
Traditional Steak Sauce

Jack Daniel's Barbecue Sauce
www.jackdanielssauces.com; 800-577-2823

Hickory Brown Sugar
Honey Smokehouse
Masterblend
Original #7
Spicy

Jack Daniel's Steak Sauce
www.jackdanielssauces.com; 800-577-2823

Original and Smokey

Kraft
www.kraftrecipes.com; 877-535-5666

Original BBQ Sauce

Condiments

B&G
www.bgfoods.com

> Pickles
> Relish
> Sauerkraut

Best Foods
www.bestfoods.com; 800-418-3275

> All

Emeril's
www.emerils.com; 800-980-8474

> Dijon Mustard
> Kicked Up Horseradish Mustard
> NY Deli Style Mustard
> Smooth Honey Mustard
> Yellow Mustard

French's
www.frenchs.com; 800-841-1256

> All Mustards

Condiments Cont'd

Heinz
www.heinz.com; 800-255-5750

Easy Squeeze Ketchup
Hot and Spicy Kick'rs
Ketchup
All Mustards
No Sodium Added Ketchup
One-Carb Ketchup

Hellmann's
www.hellmanns.us; 800-418-3275

All

Maple Syrup ***

All 100% Pure Maple Syrups

Mrs. Butterworths
www.mrsbutterworths.com

Maple Syrups

Miracle Whip
brands.kraftfoods.com/miraclewhip; 877-535-5666

All

Aisles: Oils, Sauces, and Spreads

Condiments Cont'd

Mt. Olive Pickles
www.mtolivepickles.com

All

Vlasic
www.vlasic.com

Relish and Pickles

Note

My wife and I hold on to extra condiment packets like ketchup, mustard, and dipping sauces from various restaurants. These little packets are perfect for lunches, picnics, short trips, and other outings where you may need gluten-free condiments. Amazon.com carries individual San-J Tamari Soy Sauce Travel Packs and Newman's Own salad dressing packets.

Dips

Athenos ***
www.athenos.com; 877-535-5666

All

Cookwell & Company
www.cookwell.net; 512-306-0044

Blanco Con Chile Verde Queso
Salsa Escabeche Queso

Fantastic World Foods
www.fantasticfoods.com

Original Hummus

Fritos
www.fritolay.com; 800-352-4477

Bean Dip
Chili Cheese Dip
Hot Bean Dip
Jalapeno & Cheddar Flavored Cheese Dip
Mild Cheddar Flavor Cheese
Southwest Enchilada Black Bean Flavored Dip

Dips Cont'd

Lay's
www.fritolay.com; 800-352-4477

Creamy Ranch Dip
French Onion Dip
French Onion Flavored Dry Dip Mix
Green Onion Flavored Dry Dip Mix
Heavenly Baked Potato Flavored Dip
Ranch Flavored Dry Dip Mix

Tostitos
www.fritolay.com; 800-352-4477

Monterey Jack Queso
Salsa Con Queso
Smooth & Cheesy Dip
Southwestern Ranch
Spicy Nacho
Spicy Queso Supreme
Spinach Dip
Zesty Bean & Cheese

Enchilada Sauces

La Victoria
www.lavictoria.com; 800-523-4635

   Red Enchilada Sauce Mild and Hot

Las Palmas
www.bgfoods.com

   Red Enchilada Sauce

Taco Bell
www.tacobell.com; 800-822-6235

   Taco Sauce Mild and Medium

Green Chile

505 Southwestern
www.505chile.com; 800-292-9900

    Chipotle Honey Roasted Green Chile
    Diced Flame Roasted Green Chile
    Green Chile Sauce

La Victoria
www.lavictoria.com; 800-523-4635

    Green Salsa

Note

Many traditional green chile recipes contain gluten.

Hot Sauces

Cookwell & Company
www.cookwell.net; 512-306-0044

    Mango Habanero Sweet Heat
    Pineapple Jalapeno Sweet Heat

Frank's Red Hot
www.franksredhot.com; 800-841-1256

    Buffalo Wings Sauce
    Hot Buffalo Wings Sauce
    Original
    Sweet Chili Sauce
    Sweet Heat BBQ Wings Sauce
    XTRA Hot

Heinz
www.heinz.com; 800-255-5750

    All Chili Sauces

Las Palmas
www.bgfoods.com

    Red Chili Sauce

Hot Sauces Cont'd

Trappey's
www.bgfoods.com/trappeys/trappeys_index.asp?n=10

All Hot Sauces

Marinades

Jack Daniel's EZ Marinader
www.jackdanielssauces.com; 800-577-2823

> Garlic & Herb Variety
> Steakhouse Variety
> Teriyaki Variety

Wright's Liquid Smoke
www.bgfoods.com/brand_wrights.asp

> Hickory
> Mesquite

Oils

Mazola
www.mazola.com; 800-691-1106

   All Oils

Napa Valley Naturals
www.napavalleynaturals.com; 866-972-6879

   All Oils

Other Cooking-Related

Heinz
www.heinz.com; 800-255-5750

     Cocktail Sauce
     Sloppy Joe Sauce
     Tartar Sauce
     Worcestershire Sauce

Lea & Perrins
www.leaperrins.com

     White Wine Marinade
     Worcestershire Sauce

Regina
www.reginavinegar.com

     All Cooking Wines

Pasta Sauces

Amy's
www.amys.com; 707-568-4500

> Organic Family Marinara Low Sodium
> Organic Family Marinara Pasta Sauce
> Organic Tomato Basil Low Sodium
> Organic Tomato Basil Pasta Sauce

Bertolli
www.villabertolli.com; 800-450-8699

> Alfredo

Classico
www.classico.com

> All red and white sauces

Dei Fratelli
www.deifratelli.com; 800-837-1631

> All

Muir Glenn
www.muirglen.com; 800-624-4123

> All

Pasta Sauces Cont'd

Newman's Own ***
www.newmansown.com

    All

Prego
www.prego.com; 800-257-8443

    Chunky Garden Combo
    Chunky Garden Mushroom & Green Pepper
    Chunky Garden Tomato, Onion & Garlic
    Flavored with Meat
    Fresh Mushroom
    Heart Smart Mushroom
    Heart Smart Onion & Garlic
    Heart Smart Ricotta Parmesan
    Heart Smart Roasted Red Pepper & Garlic
    Heart Smart Traditional
    Italian Sausage & Garlic
    Marinara
    Mushroom & Garlic
    Roasted Garlic & Herb
    Roasted Garlic Parmesan
    Three Cheese
    Tomato Basil Garlic
    Traditional

Pizza Sauces

Cento
www.cento.com

Fully Prepared Pizza Sauce

Enrico's
www.enricos.com; 888-472-8237

All Natural Pizza Sauce

Note

I use Newman's Own Marinara pasta sauce as pizza sauce.

Salad Dressings

Bolthouse Farms
www.bolthouse.com; 800-467-4683

　　All Salad Dressings

Cookwell & Company
www.cookwell.net; 512-306-0044

　　Cracked Black Pepper Vinaigrette
　　Italian Herb and Olive Oil Marinade
　　Olive and Lemon Vinaigrette
　　Watermelon Vinaigrette

Emeril's
www.emerils.com; 800-980-8474

　　Balsamic Vinaigrette
　　Caesar Dressing
　　House Herb Vinaigrette
　　Italian Vinaigrette
　　Raspberry Balsamic Vinaigrette

Kraft
www.kraftrecipes.com; 877-535-5666

　　Balsamic Vinaigrette
　　Buttermilk Ranch

Salad Dressings Cont'd

Kraft Cont'd

Classic Italian Vinaigrette
Free Catalina
Free Honey Dijon
Free Italian
Free Ranch Fat Free
Greek Vinaigrette
Light Creamy French Style
Light Thousand Island
Light Three Cheese Ranch
Ranch
Ranch with Bacon
Roasted Red Pepper Italian with Parmesan
Special Collection Parmesan Romano
Sweet Honey Catalina
Tangy Tomato Bacon
Thousand Island
Three Cheese Ranch
Tuscan House Italian

Newman's Own ***
www.newmansown.com

Balsamic Salad Mist
Balsamic Vinaigrette
Caesar
Creamy Caesar

Salad Dressings Cont'd

Newman's Own Cont'd

Creamy Italian
Greek
Italian Salad Mist
Light Balsamic Vinaigrette
Light Caesar
Light Cranberry Walnut
Light Honey Mustard
Light Italian
Light Lime Vinaigrette
Light Raspberry Walnut
Light Red Wine Vinegar & Olive Oil
Light Roasted Garlic Balsamic
Light Sun Dried Tomato Italian
Olive Oil & Vinegar
Orange Ginger
Organic Light Balsamic Vinaigrette
Organic Tuscan Italian
Parmesan & Roasted Garlic
Poppy Seed
Ranch
Red Wine Vinegar & Olive Oil
Southwest
Three Cheese Balsamic Vinaigrette
Two Thousand Island

Salsas

505 Southwestern
www.505chile.com; 800-292-9900

All

Amy's
www.amys.com; 707-568-4500

Organic Black Bean & Corn
Organic Medium
Organic Mild
Organic Spicy Chipotle

Cookwell & Company
www.cookwell.net; 512-306-0044

Corn and Black Bean Salsa
Escabeche Salsa
Tomatillo Salsa

Dei Fratelli
www.deifratelli.com; 800-837-1631

All

Salsas Cont'd

Green Mountain Gringo
www.greenmountaingringo.com

All

La Victoria *
www.lavictoria.com; 800-523-4635

All

Newman's Own
www.newmansown.com

Black Bean and Corn
Cilantro
Farmer's Garden
Mango
Organic Medium
Peach
Pineapple
Roasted Garlic

On the Border
www.trucoenterprises.com; 800-471-7723

All

Salsas Cont'd

TGI Friday's
www.tgifridays.com/retail/blenders; 800-374-3297

All

Tostitos
www.fritolay.com; 800-352-4477

All Natural Hot Chunky Salsa
All Natural Medium Black Bean & Corn
All Natural Medium Chunky
All Natural Medium Picante Sauce
All Natural Medium Pineapple & Peach Salsa
All Natural Mild Chunky Salsa
All Natural Mild Picante Sauce
Creamy Salsa
Restaurant Style Salsa
Sweet & Spicy Summer Salsa

Spreads

Earth Balance
www.earthbalancenatural.com; 201-421-3970

>   Almond Butter
>   Olive Oil Spread
>   Organic Spread
>   Original Spread
>   Peanut Butter
>   Soy Free Spread
>   Soy Garden Spread
>   Vegan Buttery Sticks

JIF
www.jif.com

>   All Peanut Butter products

MaraNatha
www.maranathafoods.com; 800-434-4246

>   All Nut Butters

Peanut Butter & Co. ***
www.ilovepeanutbutter.com; 866-456-8372

>   All Peanut Butters

Spreads Cont'd

Skippy
www.peanutbutter.com; 866-475-4779

> Natural (all)
> All Peanut Butter products
> All Reduced Fat
> All Roasted Honey Nut

Smucker's
www.smuckers.com; 888-550-9555

> Goober Grape
> Goober Strawberry
> Natural Chunky
> Natural Creamy
> Natural No Salt Added
> Natural Peanut Butter with Honey
> Organic Creamy and Chunky

Welch's
www.welchs.com; 800-340-6870

> All

Vinegars

Marukan Vinegar (U.S.A.) Inc.
www.marukan-usa.com; 562-630-6060

All
AVOID Soy Ponzu Dressing

Regina
www.reginavinegar.com

All Vinegars

Note

White and apple cider vinegars are generally gluten-free. Avoid malt vinegars.

Aisles:

Snacks

Candy

Dove
www.dovechocolate.com; 800-551-0704

Milk Chocolate and Dark Chocolate bars

Ferrara Pan
www.ferrapan.com; 708-366-0500

All candies

M&M's
www.m-ms.com/us; 800-627-7852

Milk Chocolate
Peanut
Peanut Butter

Milky Way
www.milkywaybar.com; 800-627-7852

Milky Way Midnight

Candy Cont'd

Necco
www.necco.com; 781-485-4500

Banana Split Chews
Canada Mint
Wintergreen Lozenges
Candy Stix
Clark Bars
Haviland Peppermint Patties
Haviland Wintergreen Patties
Mary Jane Peanut Butter Kisses
Mary Janes
Mint Julep Chews
Necco Candy Eggs
Necco Wafers
Skybars
Squirrel Nut Caramels
Squirrel Nut Zippers
Sweethearts Conversation Hearts
Talking Pumpkins
ULTRAMINTS

Candy Cont'd

Snickers
www.snickers.com; 800-627-7852

    Snickers Bar
    Snickers 2 To Go

Starburst
www.starburst.com; 800-235-2883

    Original Fruit Chews
    Original GummiBursts
    Original JellyBeans

Tootsie Roll Industries
www.tootsie.com; 773-838-3400

    All Cry Baby products
    All Double Bubble products
    Andes Mints
    Caramel Apple Pops
    Cella's Cherries
    Charleston Chew
    Charms Blow Pops, Flat Pops, Mini Pops
    Child's Play Variety Bag (all)
    Crows
    DOTS
    Fluffy Stuff Cotton Candy
    Frooties

Candy Cont'd

Tootsie Roll Industries Cont'd

Junior Mints
Nik-l-Nip
Razzles
Sugar Babies
Sugar Daddy
Tootsie Pops
Tootsie Rolls
Wack-O-Wax

Note

Regular Milky Way bars are not gluten-free. Only Milky Way Midnight is.

Around holidays like Valentine's Day and Halloween, keep some extra gluten-free candy around and trade your child one of these safe choices for any questionable or gluten-containing candy. Remember that if you don't know, you don't eat it!

Chips and Crisps

Baked Cheetos
www.fritolay.com/index.html; 800-352-4477

FLAMIN' HOT Cheese Flavored Snacks
Crunchy Cheese Flavored Snacks

Baked Doritos
www.fritolay.com/index.html; 800-352-4477

Nacho Cheese Favored Tortilla Chips

Baked! Lay's
www.fritolay.com/index.html; 800-352-4477

Cheddar & Sour Cream
Original Potato Crisps
Parmesan and Tuscan Herb
Sour Cream & Onion
Southwestern Ranch

Baked! Ruffles
www.fritolay.com/index.html; 800-352-4477

Cheddar & Sour Cream
Original Potato Crisps

Chips and Crisps Cont'd

Baked! Tostitos
www.fritolay.com/index.html; 800-352-4477

Scoops! Tortilla Chips

Baken-ets
www.fritolay.com/index.html; 800-352-4477

BBQ Flavored Fried Pork Skins
Fried Pork Skins
Hot 'N Spicy Flavored Fried Pork Cracklins
Hot 'N Spicy Flavored Pork Skins
Hot Sauce Flavored Fried Pork Cracklins

Boulder Canyon Foods ***
www.bouldercanyonfoods.com; 800-279-2250 ext. 6228

50% Reduced Salt Kettle Chips
60% Reduced Sodium Totally Natural Kettle Chips
Balsamic Vinegar & Rosemary Kettle Chips
Canyon Cut Honey BBQ Chips
Canyon Cut Salt & Cracked Pepper Potato Chips
Canyon Cut Sour Cream & Chive Potato Chips
Canyon Cut Totally Natural Potato Chips
Chipotle Ranch Kettle Chips
Hickory Barbeque Kettle Chips

Chips and Crisps Cont'd

Boulder Canyon Foods Cont'd

Jalapeno Cheddar Kettle Chips
Lightly Salted Tortilla Chips with Hummus
Limon Kettle Chips
No Salt Added Totally Natural Kettle Chips
Olive Oil Totally Natural Kettle Chips
Parmesan & Garlic Kettle Chips
Red Wine Vinegar Kettle Chips
Rice & Adzuki Bean Sundried Tomato with Basil
Artisan Snack Chips
Rice & Bean Chipotle Cheese Artisan Snack Chips
Rice & Bean Natural Salt Artisan Snack Chips
Rice & Bean Sweet Lemon & Cracked Pepper
Artisan Snack Chips
Sea Salt & Cracked Pepper Kettle Chips
Spinach & Artichoke Kettle Chips
Sweet Lemon & Cracked Pepper Kettle Chips
Tomato & Basil Kettle Chips
Tortilla Chips with Hummus & Sesame, Lightly
Salted
Totally Natural Kettle Chips

Chips and Crisps Cont'd

Cheetos
www.fritolay.com/index.html; 800-352-4477

Crunchy Cheddar Jalapeno Cheese
Crunchy Cheese
Crunchy Chile Limon
Crunchy Flamin' Hot
Crunchy Flamin' Hot Limon
Crunchy Wild Habanero
Fantastix Chili Cheese
Fantastix Flamin' Hot
Giant Puffs Flamin' Hot
Jumbo Puffs Flamin' Hot
Mighty Zingers Ragin' Cajun & Tangy Ranch
Mighty Zingers Sharp Cheddar & Salsa Picante
Twisted Cheese

Chesters
www.fritolay.com/index.html; 800-352-4477

Chili Cheese
FLAMIN' HOT

Chips and Crisps Cont'd

Doritos
www.fritolay.com/index.html; 800-352-4477

1st Degree Burn Blazin' Jalapeno
2nd Degree Burn Fiery Buffalo
Black Pepper Jack Cheese
Blazin' Buffalo & Ranch
Collisions Cheesy Enchilada & Sour Cream
Collisions Hot Wings & Blue Cheese
Collisions Pizza Cravers & Ranch
COOL RANCH
Diablo
Last Call Jalapeno Popper
Late Night All Nighter Cheeseburger
Reduced Fat COOL RANCH
Salsa Verde
Smokin' Cheddar BBQ
Spicy Nacho
Tacos at Midnight
Toasted Corn

Fritos
www.fritolay.com/index.html; 800-352-4477

SCOOPS Corn Chips
FLAVOR TWISTS Honey BBQ
Light Salted
Original
Spicy Jalapeno

Chips and Crisps Cont'd

Funyuns
www.fritolay.com/index.html; 800-352-4477

   Flamin' Hot Onion Flavored Rings
   Onion Flavored Rings

Grande Tortilla Chips
www.grandefoods.com

   Nacho Cheese Tortilla Chips
   Original Tortilla Chips
   Reduced Fat Tortilla Chips
   Restaurant Style Tortilla Chips
   Salsa Limon Tortilla Chips

Lay's
www.fritolay.com/index.html; 800-352-4477

   Balsamic Sweet Onion
   Cajun Herb & Spice
   Cheddar & Sour Cream
   STAX Cheddar
   Chile Limon
   Classic Potato Chips
   Deli Style Original
   Dill Pickle
   Garden Tomato & Basil

Chips and Crisps Cont'd

Lay's Cont'd

Honey BBQ
Hot & Spicy Barbecue
STAX Jalapeno Cheddar
Kettle Cooked Crinkle Cut BBQ
Kettle Cooked Crinkle Cut Original
Kettle Cooked Jalapeno Flavored Extra Crunchy
Kettle Cooked Original
Kettle Cooked Reduced Fat Original
Kettle Cooked Sea Salt & Cracked Pepper
Kettle Cooked Sea Salt & Vinegar
Kettle Cooked Sharp Cheddar
Kettle Cooked Sweet Chili & Sour Cream
Light Original
Lightly Salted
Limon Tangy Lime
STAX Mesquite Barbecue
Natural Sea Salt Thick Cut
STAX Original
Pepper Relish
STAX Ranch

Chips and Crisps Cont'd

Lay's Cont'd

    Salt & Vinegar
    Sour Cream & Onion
    Southwest Cheese & Chilies
    Sweet & Spicy Buffalo Wing
    Sweet Southern Heat BBQ
    Tangy Carolina BBQ
    Wavy Au Gratin
    Wavy Hickory BBQ
    Wavy Ranch
    Wavy Regular

Lundberg Rice Chips
www.lundberg.com; 530-882-4551

    Fiesta Lime
    Honey Dijon
    Nacho Cheese
    Pico de Gallo
    Santa Fe Barbecue
    Sea Salt
    Sesame & Seaweed
    Wasabi

Chips and Crisps Cont'd

Maui Style
www.fritolay.com/index.html; 800-352-4477

 Regular Potato Chips
 Salt & Vinegar

Miss Vickie's
www.fritolay.com; 800-352-4477

 Hand Picked Jalapeno Kettle Cooked
 Sea Salt & Cracked Pepper
 Sea Salt & Vinegar Kettle Cooked
 Smokehouse BBQ Kettle Cooked

Mr. Krispers
www.mrkrispers.com

 All Crisps

Munchos
www.fritolay.com; 800-352-4477

 Regular Potato Chips

Chips and Crisps Cont'd

Ruffles
www.fritolay.com; 800-352-4477

Authentic Barbecue
Cheddar & Sour Cream
Light Original
Lightly Salted
Natural Reduced Fat Sea Salted
Original
Queso Flavored
Reduced Fat Original
Sour Cream & Onion

Sabritas
www.fritolay.com; 800-352-4477

Adobadas
Chile Piquin
Habanero Limon
Rancheritos
Turbos Flamas
White Corn Restaurant Style
Yellow Corn Tortilla

Chips and Crisps Cont'd

Tostitos
www.fritolay.com; 800-352-4477

Bite Size Rounds Tortilla Chips
Blue Corn Restaurant Style
Crispy Rounds
Dipping Strips
Natural Blue Corn Restaurant Style
Natural Yellow Corn Restaurant Style
Restaurant Style with a Hint of Lime Flavor
Salsa Verde
SCOOPS! Hint of Jalapeno
SCOOPS! Regular

Cookies

Annie's
www.annies.com; 800 288-1089

    Gluten Free Bunny Cookies

Ener-G Foods
www.ener-g.com; 800-331-5222

    Biscotti Chocolate Chip Cookies
    Biscotti Raisin Cookies
    Chocolate Chip Potato Cookies
    Chocolate Chip Snack Bars
    Chocolate Cookies
    Cinnamon Cookies
    Ginger Cookies
    Sunflower Cookies
    Vanilla Cookies
    White Chocolate Chip Cookies

Ians
www.iansnaturalfoods.com; 800-543-6637

    Gluten Free Chocolate Chip Cookie Buttons
    Gluten Free Cinnamon Cookie Buttons

Cookies Cont'd

Mary's Gone Crackers
www.marysgonecrackers.com; 888-258-1250

Chocolate Chip Cookies
Double Chocolate Chip Cookies
Ginger Snap Cookies
N' Oatmeal Raisin Cookies

Mi-Del ***
www.midelcookies.com

Gluten-Free Arrowroot Cookies
Gluten-Free Chocolate Chip
Gluten-Free Chocolate Sandwiches
Gluten-Free Cinnamon Snaps
Gluten-Free Ginger Snaps
Gluten-Free Pecan
Gluten-Free Royal Vanilla Sandwiches

Schar
www.schar.com/us

Petit Biscuits
Twin Bar
Wafer Pocket

Crackers

Blue Diamond *
www.bluediamond.com; 800-987-2329

Almond Nut-Thins
BBQ Nut-Thins
Cheddar Cheese Nut-Thins
Country Ranch Nut-Thins
Hazelnut Nut-Thins
Hint of Sea Salt Nut-Thins
Pecan Nut-Thins
Smokehouse Nut-Thins

Crunchmaster *
www.crunchmaster.com; 800-896-2396

Multi-Grain Crackers
Multi-Seed Crackers
Rice Crackers

Ener-G Foods
www.ener-g.com; 800-331-5222

Cinnamon Crackers
Ener-G Gourmet Crackers
Seattle Crackers

Crackers Cont'd

Glutino
www.glutino.com; 800-363-3438

Gluten Free Cheddar Crackers
Gluten Free Original Crackers
Multigrain Crackers
Vegetable Crackers

Mary's Gone Crackers ***
www.marysgonecrackers.com; 888-258-1250

Black Pepper Crackers
Caraway Crackers
Herb Crackers
Onion Crackers
Original Seed Cracker

Crackers Cont'd

Schar
www.schar.com/us

    Cialde Wafer
    Crackers
    Crackers Pocket
    Crisp Rolls
    Fette Biscottate
    Fette Croccanti
    Funkies
    Grissini
    Salinis
    Salti

Aisles: Snacks

Fruit Snacks

Annie's
www.annies.com; 800 288-1089

Organic Bunny Fruit Snacks

Betty Crocker
www.bettycrocker.com; 800-446-1898

Fruit by the Foot
Fruit Flavored Shapes
Fruit Gushers
Fruit Roll-Ups

Del Monte
www.delmonte.com; 800-543-3090

All Fruit Cups

Dole
www.dole.com; 800-356-3111

All Fruit Cups

Fruit Snacks Cont'd

Musselman's
www.musselmans.com; 717-677-8181

Chunky Apple Sauce
Cinnamon Apple Sauce
Healthy Picks Blueberry
Healthy Picks Cupucacu Key Lime
Healthy Picks Pomegranate
Healthy Picks Raspberry Acai
Organic Sweetened and Unsweetened Apple Sauce
Sesame Street Fruit-Flavored Apple Sauces
Sweetened Apple Sauce
Totally Fruit Apple
Totally Fruit Mixed Berry
Totally Fruit Peach
Totally Fruit Strawberry

Welch's ***
www.welchs.com; 800-340-6870

All fruit snacks

Nuts

Blue Diamond ***
www.bluediamond.com; 800-987-2329

Bold Blazin' Buffalo Wing
Bold Carolina Barbecue
Bold Habanero BBQ
Bold Jalapeno Smokehouse
Bold Lime 'n Chili
Bold Salt 'n Vinegar
Honey Roasted Almonds
Lightly Salted Almonds
Roasted Salted Almonds
Smokehouse Almonds
Whole Natural Almonds

Frito-Lay
www.fritolay.com; 800-352-4477

Cashews
Deluxe Mixed Nuts
Honey Roasted Peanuts
Hot Peanuts
Nut & Chocolate Trail Mix
Nut & Fruit Trail Mix
Original Trail Mix
Praline Pecans
Salted Peanuts
Smoked Almonds

Nuts Cont'd

Nut Harvest
www.fritolay.com; 800-352-4477

      Natural Lightly Roasted Almonds
      Natural Nut & Fruit Mix
      Natural Sea Salted Peanuts
      Natural Sea Salted Whole Cashews

Planters
www.planters.com; 800-323-0768

      Cocktail Peanuts (Regular, Lightly Salted, and Unsalted)
      Dry Roasted (Regular, Lightly Salted, and Unsalted)
      Honey & Dry Roasted
      Honey Roasted
      Redskin Spanish Peanuts
      Sweet & Crunchy

Sabritas
www.fritolay.com; 800-352-4477

      Picante Peanuts
      Salt & Lime Peanuts

Nuts Cont'd

True North
www.fritolay.com; 800-352-4477

Almond Clusters
Almond Cranberry Vanilla Clusters
Almond Cranberry Vanilla Clusters in White
Chocolate
Almond Pecan Cashew Clusters
Almonds Pistachios
Citrus Burst Nut Clusters
Pecan Almond Peanut Clusters
Walnuts Pecans

Popcorns and Puffs

Cheetos
www.fritolay.com; 800-352-4477

   Giant Puffs
   Natural White Cheddar Puffs
   Puffs
   Butter Flavored Puffcorn
   Flamin' Hot

Cracker Jack
www.crackerjack.com; 800-352-4477

   Original Caramel Coated Popcorn & Peanuts

Smartfood
www.fritolay.com; 800-352-4477

   Cranberry Almond
   Peanut Butter Apple
   Reduced Fat White Cheddar
   White Cheddar

Pretzels and Sticks

Ener-G Foods
www.ener-g.com; 800-331-5222

     Ener-G Pretzels
     Sesame Pretzel Rings
     Wylde Pretzels
     Wylde Pretzel Rings

Mary's Gone Crackers
www.marysgonecrackers.com; 888-258-1250

     Sticks and Twigs–Chipotle Tomato
     Sticks and Twigs–Curry
     Sticks and Twigs–Sea Salt

Snyder's of Hanover
www.snydersofhanover.com

     Gluten Free Pretzel Sticks

Rice Cakes

Lundberg Family Farms ***
www.lundberg.com; 530-882-4551

Brown Rice, Lightly Salted
Brown Rice, Salt Free
Caramel Corn
Cinnamon Toast
Eco Farmed Apple Cinnamon
Eco Farmed Brown Rice, Lightly Salted
Eco Farmed Brown Rice, Salt Free
Eco Farmed Buttery Caramel
Eco Farmed Honey Nut
Eco Farmed Sesame Tamari
Eco Farmed Toasted Sesame
Flax with Tamari
Koku Seaweed
Mochi Sweet
Popcorn
Sesame Tamari
Sweet Green Tea with Lemon
Tamari with Seaweed
Wild Rice, Lightly Salted

Mother's Natural
www.mothersnatural.com; 800-333-8142

All Rice Cakes

Seeds

Frito-Lay
www.fritolay.com; 800-352-4477

Ranch Sunflower Seeds
Sunflower Seed Kernels
Sunflower Seeds

Spitz
www.fritolay.com; 800-352-4477

Chili Lime Sunflower Seeds
Cracked Pepper Sunflower Seeds
Dill Pickle Sunflower Seeds
Salted Sunflower Seeds
Seasoned Pumpkin Seeds
Seasoned Sunflower Seeds
Smoky BBQ Sunflower Seeds
Spicy Sunflower Seeds

Snack Bars

Ians
www.iansnaturalfoods.com; 800-543-6637

    Gluten Free Go Bars: Apple Pie
    Gluten Free Go Bars: Cinnamon Bun

KIND
www.kindsnacks.com; 212-616-3006

    All flavors

LÄRABAR
www.larabar.com; 720-945-1155

    All flavors

Nature's Path
www.naturespath.com; 888-808-9505

    Envirokids Organic Cheetah Berry Crispy Rice Bars
    Envirokids Organic Fruity Burst Crispy Rice Bars
    Envirokids Organic Koala Chocolate Crispy Rice Bars
    Envirokids Organic Peanut Butter Crispy Rice Bars
    Envirokids Organic Peanut Choco Drizzle Crispy
    Rice Bars

Index